Celine

Behind the Music,   Beyond the Voice

(A Biography)

Leticia Allison

Table of Contents

Introduction

Chapter 1: Early Life

> Family Ties and Humble Upbringing
> A Musical Prodigy in the Making

Chapter 2: Rise to Fame

> "La voix du bon Dieu": A Precocious
> Debut
> Conquering Canada: Success in the
> Canadian Music Industry
> The Self-Titled Album "Celine Dion"
> and Global Stardom

Chapter 3: Personal life

> A Remarkable Beginning
> Love Blossoms: Marriage and Family
> The Heartbreaking Loss: René Angélil's
> Passing in 2016
> A Legacy of Love and Music

Chapter 4: Health

> Anxiety and Depression: Behind the
> Spotlight

The Diagnosis: Stiff Person Syndrome
Impact on Career and Personal Life
A Legacy of Resilience

Chapter 5: Career highlights
Chart-Topping Albums and Singles
Grammy Awards: A Record-Breaking
Success
Las Vegas Resident: A Landmark
Achievement

Chapter 6: Legacy
Vocal Virtuosity: A Standard of
Excellence
Breaking Language Barriers: A Global
Sensation
A Trailblazer for Balladry and Emotional
Depth
Influence on Popular Culture
Enduring Popularity and Timeless
Appeal

Conclusion

Introduction

Celine Dion: A Vocal Powerhouse

Celine Dion, the Canadian songstress, has not only captured the hearts of millions with her ethereal voice but has also become an iconic figure in the world of music. Born on March 30, 1968, in Charlemagne, Quebec, Dion's extraordinary talent was evident from a young age. Her journey from a small-town girl to an international sensation is nothing short of remarkable.

At just 12 years old, Dion recorded her first English-language album, setting the stage for a career that would span decades. Her 1997 hit, "My Heart Will Go On, " from the blockbuster film Titanic, catapulted her to global stardom and remains one of the best-selling singles of all time. With a record-breaking residency in Las Vegas, numerous awards including Grammy's and an Academy Award, Celine Dion's impact on the music industry is undeniable.

Prepare to delve into the riveting tale of a woman whose voice transcends borders and whose journey is an inspiration to aspiring artists worldwide. This is the story of Celine Dion, a force to be reckoned with in the realm of music and a testament to the power of unwavering passion and dedication.

Chapter 1: Early Life

In the heart of Quebec, Canada, nestled in the charming town of Charlemagne, a star was born on March 30, 1968. Celine Dion, the youngest of fourteen siblings, had a childhood that was as humble as it was filled with love. Her journey from modest beginnings to becoming a global music sensation is a captivating tale of talent, perseverance, and unwavering family support.

Family Ties and Humble Upbringing

Celine Marie Claudette Dion was the youngest child of Adhémar Dion and Thérèse Tanguay. Her family's roots were deeply embedded in the picturesque town of Charlemagne, where they ran a small but close-knit family business. The Dion household, while large, was characterized by the warmth and unity that comes with shared dreams and ambitions. Despite the financial challenges that often accompany raising a family of such size, the Dion's instilled strong values of hard work and determination in their children.

The tight bond between Between Celine and her siblings was evident from an early age. Their home, though simple, resonated with laughter and song. This close-knit environment provided the perfect backdrop for the budding star's early years, nurturing her talent and laying the foundation for a remarkable future.

A Musical Prodigy in the Making

It wasn't long before Celine's extraordinary talent began to shine through. At the tender age of five, she was already belting out tunes with a voice that defied her years. Her family recognized her gift and wholeheartedly supported her budding musical aspirations. Her brother, Michel, even crafted a makeshift stage in their home's basement, where Celine would practice her singing, performing for an audience of enthusiastic siblings.

Celine's musical inclinations were nurtured by her mother, Thérèse, who played a pivotal role in fostering her early interest in music. Thérèse's love for the arts and her encouragement propelled Colin's passion to new heights. Under her mother's guidance, Celine honed her skills, learning to read music and developing her vocal range.

As the family recognized Celine's prodigious talent, they made considerable sacrifices to support her burgeoning career. Her parents mortgaged their home to finance her first album, "La voix du bon Dieu, " when she was just 12 years old. It was a bold move that would prove to be a pivotal step towards her future stardom.

Celine's upbringing was marked by a remarkable fusion of talent and familial devotion. Her family's unwavering support, both emotionally and financially, allowed her to develop the skills and confidence necessary to embark on her journey to stardom. With her roots firmly grounded in Charlemagne, Quebec, Celine Dion's early years in this small Canadian town set the stage for her ascent to international acclaim.

Celine Dion's exceptional childhood in Charlemagne, Quebec, was a harmonious blend of family bonds and musical passion. Her story serves as a testament to the power of familial support and determination, proving that from humble beginnings, a global superstar can emerge. It was in the heart of Charlemagne that the seeds of her remarkable journey were down, eventually blossoming into a legacy that continues to inspire aspiring artists and music lovers worldwide.

Chapter 2: Rise to Fame

Celine Dion's ascent to international superstardom is a tale of sheer talent, unwavering determination, and a series of pivotal moments. Among these, her early breakthrough with the song "La voix du bon Dieu" marked the inception of a remarkable career. Let's explore how this young Canadian sensation not only conquered the hearts of her compatriots but also ventured into the global stage with her self-titled album "Celine Dion. "

"La voix du bon Dieu": A Precocious Debut

In the annals of music history, Celine Dion's debut album, "La voix du bon Dieu, " remains an unforgettable milestone. Released in 1981 when she was just 12 years old, this album was a testament to Celine's remarkable talent and her family's unwavering support. The title track,   "La voix du bon Dieu,   " became an instant hit in Quebec and showcased to the world a voice that was truly a gift from the heavens.

The album's success can be attributed to Celine's soul-stirring vocals and the heartfelt lyrics she sang with a depth that blind her age. It quickly became a sensation in French-speaking Canada,   establishing her as a rising star in the local music scene.   In the years that followed,   she would go on to release several more French-language albums, solidifying her presence in the Canadian music industry.

Conquering Canada: Success in the Canadian Music Industry

Celine Dion's journey to stardom within her home country was not without its challenges. In a competitive Canadian music landscape, she had to work tirelessly to prove herself. Her determination to succeed was underpinned by her family's sacrifices, notably her parents mortgaging their home to finance "La voix du bon Dieu. "

The success of this album was a stepping stone that allowed Celine to make her mark in the Canadian music industry. Her early records showcase her formidable vocal range and a depth of emotion that resonated with audiences. She was recognized with numerous awards, including Félix Awards and Juno Awards, solidifying her reputation as a talented and promising artist.

As Colin's career continued to evolve, she also branched into the English-speaking market. Her transition to English-language music was a pivotal moment in her career, and it laid the foundation for her eventual international breakthrough.

The Self-Titled Album "Celine Dion" and Global Stardom

In 1990, Celine Dion released a self-titled English-language album that would redefine her career. With tracks like "Where Does My Heart Beat Now, " the album showcased her remarkable vocal prowess and marked the beginning of her international journey. Her commitment to excellence and her flawless delivery let her apart from the competition.

However, it was her rendition of the song for Disney's animated film "Beauty and the Beast" that catapulted her to global stardom. The song, also titled "Beauty and the Beast, " was a duet with Peabo Bryson and won both a Grammy and an Academy Award. This achievement not only garnered her international recognition but also introduced her to a broader, worldwide audience.

The success of her self-titled album and the song from "Beauty and the Beast" were pivotal in Celine's transition from a Canadian sensation to a global icon. Her powerful voice and undeniable talent transcended borders, capturing the hearts of fans around the world. In the years that followed, Celine Dion would go on to release a series of chart-topping albums and singles, solidifying her status as one of the most celebrated and enduring artists in the history of music.

Celine Dion's journey from the debut of "La voix du bon Dieu" to the global phenomenon she is today is a testament to her exceptional talent, relentless dedication, and unwavering family support. Her remarkable success in the Canadian music industry paved the way for her international breakthrough, and her self-titled album "Celine Dion" served as the catalyst that propelled her to worldwide stardom. Her journey is a source of inspiration for aspiring artists, a true testament to the power of passion and the indomitable spirit of an extraordinary artist.

Chapter 3: Personal life

The story of Celine Dion's relationship with René Angélil is a tale of love, partnership, and unwavering support that transcended both their personal and professional lives. From their early beginnings to the heartbreaking loss of Angélil in 2016, their journey together is a testament to the enduring power of love.

A Remarkable Beginning

Celine Dion first crossed paths with René Angélil when she was just 12 years old. Angélil, a respected music manager, and producer, was captivated by the young singer's talent and potential during a meeting at his office in Montreal. He was so moved by her voice that he decided to take a monumental step in nurturing her career. This marked the start of a professional relationship that would eventually evolve into a profound personal connection.

René Angélil recognized Celine's potential and mortgaged his own house to finance her debut album,   "La voix du bon Dieu.   " He became her manager and played an integral role in shaping her career.   Their professional partnership quickly transformed into a deep personal connection,   and their love story began to unfold.

Love Blossoms: Marriage and Family

The romantic relationship between Celine Dion and René Angélil eventually blossomed, transcending the boundaries of manager and artist.   Despite a significant age difference, they fell deeply in love.   Their relationship was kept private for some time,   but they couldn't hide their affection for each other.   In

1994, Celine publicly announced their engagement, and the couple married on December 17 of the same year in a lavish ceremony at Notre-Dame Basilica in Montreal.

Their love story was more than just a marriage; it was a partnership in every sense of the word. René Angélil continued to manage Celine's career, guiding her to international stardom. Their family grew with the birth of their first child, René-Charles, in 2001. Their bond was unbreakable, not just as spouses but also as devoted parents.

As Celine Dion's career reached new heights, René Angélil remained a steadfast source of support. He was not just her manager but her confidant, her rock, and the person who believed in her from the very beginning. Their enduring love was a testament to the strength of their relationship, one that had weathered the challenges of fame and success.

The Heartbreaking Loss: René Angélil's Passing in 2016

The world was left in shock and mourning when, on January 14, 2016, René Angélil passed away at the age of 73. He had been battling throat cancer for several years, and his passing marked the end of an era in Celine Dion's life.

René's death was a profound loss not only for Celine but for the music industry. He had played a pivotal role in shaping her career and was her lifelong partner. Celine grieved deeply for the love of her life, and her fans mourned alongside her.

In a heartbreaking period, Celine took a temporary hiatus from her career to be with her family and to cope with the immense loss. Her courage and grace during this challenging time served as an inspiration to many who admired her not just for her music but for her strength as well.

A Legacy of Love and Music

Celine Dion and René Angélil's relationship was a love story for the ages. Their enduring love, which began as a professional partnership, evolved into a deep personal connection that resulted in a cherished marriage and family. Their bond was a testament to the strength of love, transcending age and defying industry norms.

René Angélil's passing in 2016 marked a turning point in Celine Dion's life. It was a profound loss,   but it also served as a reminder of the enduring power of love.   Celine's strength during this period,   as she continued to honor her late husband's memory while navigating her career,   showcased her resilience and unwavering commitment to their shared dreams.

The legacy of Celine Dion and René Angélil is not only one of incredible music but also a story of love and partnership that left an indelible mark on the hearts of their fans.   Their story serves as a timeless reminder that love,   when nurtured with dedication and shared dreams, can overcome all challenges and create a lasting legacy.

Chapter 4: Health

Celine Dion is renowned not only for her extraordinary vocal talent but also for her unyielding determination to overcome adversity. Over the years, the iconic singer has faced various health challenges, including anxiety, depression, and a particularly rare and debilitating condition known as Stiff Person Syndrome. In this exploration, we will delve into her journey, from the mental health struggles she encountered to her diagnosis of Stiff Person Syndrome in 2018 and the profound impact these health issues had on both her career and personal life.

Anxiety and Depression: Behind the Spotlight

While Celine Dion's public image exudes grace and confidence, her life has not been without its personal trials.   The pressures of a demanding career,   global fame,   and personal losses took their toll on her mental health.   In the early 2000s,   she revealed that she had been grappling with both anxiety and depression.

The unrelenting demands of her career, especially during her long-running Las Vegas resident,   and the emotional turmoil resulting from the loss of her husband René Angélil in 2016   undoubtedly   contributed   to   these challenges.   Celine,   in a bid to cope with these struggles,   shared her vulnerability with the world,   humanizing the experience of mental health issues for her fans.

Her openness about her battles with anxiety and depression was a significant step in reducing the stigma associated with mental health.   It also served as an inspiration to many who face similar challenges, reminding them that even the brightest stars can struggle with inner darkness.

The Diagnosis: Stiff Person Syndrome

In 2018, Celine Dion faced another health challenge, one far less common and more mysterious than the typical ailments. She was diagnosed with Stiff Person Syndrome, a rare neurological disorder that affects the muscles and often leads to stiffness, muscle spasms, and debilitating pain. This condition can severely restrict mobility and make the most basic daily activities a considerable challenge.

The diagnosis was a life-altering moment for Celine. Stiff Person Syndrome is so rare that it affects only a handful of people worldwide. Managing this condition would be a daunting task for anyone, let alone a globally renowned artist whose career was built on her stage presence and vocal prowess.

Impact on Career and Personal Life

Celine Dion's health challenges have had a significant impact on her career and personal life.   Her battles with anxiety and depression, while physically debilitating,   undoubtedly affected her ability to perform and maintain the grueling schedule that comes with global stardom.   These mental health challenges prompted her to take breaks from her career to prioritize her well-being,   showing that the brightest stars need to take care of their mental health.

The diagnosis of Stiff Person Syndrome, however,   presented a different set of challenges.   This rare and incurable condition caused muscle rigidity and spasms,   making it incredibly difficult for Celine to move freely. It was a stark contrast to the dynamic and energetic performer that the world had come to know.

Colin's health issues, especially Stiff Person Syndrome, forced her to postpone and cancel shows, disappointing fans and causing financial setbacks. Her team and family have been incredibly supportive, allowing her to adapt her performances to her physical limitations. It was a testament to her tenacity that she continued to perform despite obstacles.

On a personal level, her health challenges had a profound impact on her family life. Celine was not only dealing with her own health struggles but also raising her three children as a single mother after the loss of her husband, René Angélil. Her resilience and determination to be there for her children, while dealing with her health issues, was a testament to her strength.

A Legacy of Resilience

Celine Dion's journey through mental health issues, including anxiety and depression, and her diagnosis of Stiff Person Syndrome are a testament to her remarkable resilience. Despite the setbacks and challenges she faced, she continued to pursue her passion for music, adapt her performances, and inspire millions of fans with her indomitable spirit.

Her candidness about mental health challenges helped reduce the stigma surrounding these issues and demonstrated that they can affect anyone, regardless of their success or fame. Her journey through Stiff Person Syndrome is a testament to her strength and determination to not be defined by her health condition.

As Celine Dion continues to inspire audiences with her music, she also serves as a source of inspiration for anyone facing health challenges. Her legacy is not just one of vocal talent but also one of resilience, demonstrating that with determination and the right support, even the most formidable obstacles can be overcome. Colin's journey is a shining example of the human spirit's ability to triumph over adversity, reminding us all that, in the face of health challenges, resilience can be your greatest strength.

Chapter 5: Career highlights

Celine Dion's extraordinary career in the music industry is characterized by a string of chart-topping albums and singles that have left an indelible mark on the world of music. From her record-breaking success at the Grammy Awards to her iconic Las Vegas residency,   let's dive into the highlights of her remarkable journey,   celebrating her most successful albums and singles that have captivated the hearts of millions.

Chart-Topping Albums and Singles

Celine Dion's discography is a treasure trove of chart-topping albums and singles,   showcasing her remarkable vocal prowess and versatility. One of her early successes was the album "Unison,   " released in 1990,   which included the hit single "The Power of Love.   "

The song became a global sensation, reaching the top of the charts in numerous countries and solidifying Celine's presence in the international music scene.

In 1992, Celine released "Celine Dion, " an album that marked her entry into the English-language music market. It featured the chart-topping hit "Beauty and the Beast, " a duet with Peabo Bryson that became the theme song for the Disney film of the same name. The song won both a Grammy and an Academy Award, propelling her to international stardom.

Her 1996 album "Falling into You" was a massive success, earning her two Grammy Awards for Album of the Year and Best Pop Vocal Album. The album's standout single, "Because You Loved Me, " also reached the top of the charts and became a beloved ballad.

However, it was her 1997 album, "Let's Talk About Love, " that produced one of her most iconic songs, "My Heart Will Go On. " The song, featured in the blockbuster film Titanic, became one of the best-selling singles of all time. Colin's powerful vocals and the emotional resonance of the song struck a chord with audiences worldwide, cementing her status as a music legend.

The year 2002 saw the release of "A New Day Has Come, " an album that included hit singles like the title track and "I'm Alive. " These songs showcased her ability to captivate audiences with both ballads and upbeat tracks, further expanding her musical repertoire.

Celine Dion's career has also been defined by her ability to reinterpret and pay homage to timeless classics. Her album "These Are

Special Times, " released in 1998, featured iconic Christmas songs such as "O Holy Night" and "The Prayer, " a duet with Andrea Bocelli.

Her album "Taking Chances" (2007) displayed her continued evolution as an artist, incorporating elements of rock and pop. The title track, "Taking Chances, " exemplified her adaptability and willingness to experiment with different musical genres.

In 2013, Celine released "Loved Me Back to Life, " an album that showcased her resilience and ability to make a triumphant return to the music scene after personal challenges. The title track and singles like "Incredible" demonstrated her unwavering vocal prowess.

Celine's ability to consistently deliver chart-topping albums and singles throughout her career is a testament to her enduring talent and universal appeal. Her music has transcended genres and generations, leaving an indelible mark on the music industry.

Grammy Awards: A Record-Breaking Success

Celine Dion's accomplishments at the Grammy Awards are nothing short of extraordinary. Her powerful vocals and timeless music have earned her numerous Grammy accolades, making her one of the most celebrated artists in the history of the awards.

One of her most significant Grammy achievements came in 1996 when she won the prestigious Album of the Year award for "Falling into You. " This victory was a pivotal moment in her career and solidified her status as a global music icon.

In addition to Album of the Year, Celine has received multiple Grammy Awards in various categories, including Best Female Pop Vocal Performance, Best Pop Collaboration with Vocals, and Best Song Written for Visual Media. Her song "My Heart Will Go On" from the Titanic soundtrack won the Grammy for Record of the Year in 1999, further emphasizing her exceptional contributions to the music world.

Colin's enduring success at the Grammy Awards is a testament to her unparalleled vocal talent and her ability to connect with audiences on a profound emotional level. Her music has left an indelible mark on the world of music, earning her a well-deserved place among the Grammy greats.

Las Vegas Resident: A Landmark Achievement

In 2003, Celine Dion embarked on a groundbreaking Las Vegas residency at Caesars Palace, a movie that would redefine the concept of entertainment in the city. Her residency, titled "A New Day. . . , " was a monumental achievement in the entertainment industry.

The show featured an elaborate set, stunning visuals, and, of course, Celine's powerhouse vocals. It became a must-see event, attracting fans from all over the world. "A New Day. . . " was a testament to Celine's ability to combine her musical artistry with a larger-than-life production, setting new standards for live performances in Las Vegas.

Colin's Las Vegas resident was not just a series of concerts; it was a transformative experience that showcased her versatility as an artist. The show ran for an impressive five years, with over 700 performances, making it one of the most successful residencies in Las Vegas history.

Her residency's impact extended beyond the stage, influencing a new wave of artists who recognized the potential of Las Vegas as a hub for world-class entertainment. Celine Dion's resident remains a landmark achievement in her career and a testament to her ability to innovate and captivate audiences in new and exciting ways.

Celine Dion's career has been defined by a remarkable catalog of chart-topping albums and singles, a record-breaking journey at the Grammy Awards, and a groundbreaking Las

Vegas resident.   Her music has touched the hearts of millions,   and her influence in the music industry continues to shine as bright as her iconic performances.   Celine Dion's legacy is one of exceptional artistry,   unwavering dedication,   and the ability to create music that transcends time and resonates with audiences around the world.

Chapter 6: Legacy

Celine Dion's impact on the music industry is nothing short of monumental. Her unparalleled vocal prowess, combined with her ability to convey deep emotion through song, has made her a true force in the world of music. With a career spanning decades, she has not only set records and earned accolades but has also left an indelible mark on popular culture, influencing artists across genres and generations.

Vocal Virtuosity: A Standard of Excellence

One cannot discuss Celine Dion's impact on the music industry without acknowledging her extraordinary vocal talent. Her voice is a marvel, possessing a range and power that few artists can match. Whether belting out a powerful ballad or delivering a tender, heartfelt lyric, Colin's ability to convey raw emotion through her voice is unparalleled.

Her technical proficiency, control, and ability to effortlessly transition between octaves have set a standard of excellence in the industry. Her vocal prowess has not only earned her critical acclaim but has also resonated with audiences on a profound level. Celine Dion's voice has become synonymous with musical excellence, inspiring aspiring artists and garnering admiration from fellow musicians around the world.

Breaking Language Barriers: A Global Sensation

Celine Dion's ability to transcend linguistic boundaries is a testament to the universal appeal of her music. While she hails from the

French-speaking province of Quebec, Canada, her foray into English-language music catapulted her to global stardom. Her seamless transition between French and English albums showcased her versatility as an artist, allowing her to reach audiences on a global scale.

Her English-language albums, starting with the self-titled "Celine Dion" in 1992, demonstrated her adaptability and ability to connect with a broader audience. The success of singles like "The Power of Love, " "Because You Loved Me, " and the iconic "My Heart Will Go On" from the Titanic soundtrack further solidified her status as an international sensation.

Simultaneously, her French-language albums maintained a dedicated fan base, especially in Francophone regions around the world. Her ability to convey emotion and meaning in multiple languages speaks to her exceptional artistry and her gift for connecting with audiences on a deeply personal level, regardless of their native tongue.

A Trailblazer for Balladry and Emotional Depth

Celine Dion's impact on the music industry is perhaps most profoundly felt in her contributions to the ballad genre. Her ability to infuse songs with emotional resonance has set a standard for balladry in modern music. Whether expressing love, loss, or triumph, Colin's delivery is nothing short of transformative.

Her interpretation of songs like "The Power of Love, " "Because You Loved Me, " and "All By Myself" have become definitive versions, earning her a place among the greatest interpreters of popular ballads. Her ability to evoke powerful emotions in her audience is a hallmark of her artistry,   creating a timeless quality in her music that continues to resonate with listeners of all ages.

Influence on Popular Culture

Celine Dion's influence on popular culture extends far beyond her music.   Her signature style,   characterized by elegant yet daring fashion choices,   has made her a fashion icon. Her presence at red carpet events and fashion shows is eagerly anticipated,   with designers to collaborate with her.

Her impact on cinema is also noteworthy, particularly through her contributions to film soundtracks.   "My Heart Will Go On" from the Titanic soundtrack remains one of the most iconic songs in cinematic history, forever linked to the epic romance of Jack and Rose. The song's success not only contributed to the film's cultural impact but also solidified Celine's status as a household name.

Furthermore, Celine Dion's philanthropic efforts have endeared her to fans and admirers worldwide. Her charitable work, including her support for medical research, disaster relief, and children's causes, exemplifies her commitment to making a positive impact on the world beyond the realm of music.

Enduring Popularity and Timeless Appeal

Celine Dion's enduring popularity is a testament to the timelessness of her music and the depth of her connection with her audience. Her ability to resonate with listeners across generations is a rare gift that speaks to the universal themes she addresses in her songs.

Her influence continues to be felt in the music industry, with contemporary artists often citing her as an inspiration. Her impact on vocal technique, emotional delivery, and stage presence is evident in the work of artists who have followed in her footsteps.

Even as music trends evolve, Celine Dion remains a beloved figure, with a dedicated fan base that spans the globe. Her concerts continue to draw sold-out crowds, showcasing the enduring power of her music to captivate audiences.

Celine Dion's impact on the music industry is one of profound significance. Her vocal virtuosity, ability to convey deep emotion, and transcendent appeal have solidified her as a true icon.   Her influence on popular culture, from fashion to film,   is a testament to her status as a global phenomenon.   With an enduring popularity that shows no signs of waning,   Celine Dion's legacy as a musical trailblazer and cultural icon is firmly etched in the annals of music history.

Conclusion

In conclusion,   the life and accomplishments of Celine Dion stand as a testament to the power of talent,   determination,   and unwavering dedication.   From her humble beginnings in Charlemagne,   Quebec,   she emerged as a global music sensation, captivating audiences with her unparalleled vocal prowess and ability to convey deep emotions through song.

Colin's influence extends beyond the realms of music,   fashion,   and film.   Her philanthropic efforts and her ability to connect with fans on a profoundly personal level have solidified her legacy as not just a music icon but also as a humanitarian and an inspiration to artists worldwide.

Her enduring popularity and the timeless appeal of her music continue to resonate with audiences of all ages.   Celine Dion's legacy is one of enduring significance in the annals of the music industry,   and her voice will continue to echo in the hearts of generations to come.

Printed in Great Britain
by Amazon